ÈDÌDÀRÉ

By

Rotimi Ogunjobi

ISBN 978-978-49837-4-7

Lagos Literary and Arts Journal Imprint

© 2012 Rotimi Ogunjobi

Rotimi Ogunjobi

All rights reserved. No part of this book may be used or reproduced in any manner whatsoever without written permission, except in the case of brief quotations embodied in critical articles or reviews.

Trade and purchase details:
Published by xceedia (media and publishing)
publishing@xceedia.co.uk

Author's note and acknowledgement

Èdìdàré is a poem which tells the story of a group of adventurers in search of the *Wisdom Fruit* from the *Tree of Enlightenment*. The title and some characters were taken from books written in Yoruba by the late Yoruba author D.O Fagunwa.

This book is a work of fiction. Any similarities to persons, dead or alive, or to any place occur in the reader's mind; not mine.

CONTENTS

7	The Quest
12	The Journey
17	Edidare
30	The King's Palace
36	The Betrayal of Atanpako
39	Omugodimeta
41	The Court of Edidare
54	The Departure
56	Literal Translations

Rotimi Ogunjobi

Edidare

THE QUEST

Beyond *Oke Langbodo* of ancient legend revived;
Beyond the *Sanguine Stream* of ancient legend revived,
Near the other world where the dead go to live.
Lies that distant city, where wisdom never fades.

Beyond the enchanted forest of *Elegbeje,*
Where dwellers observe the daily doings,
Of those that have passed away into the other world,
You can daily hear the sable roosters crow at dawn,
From across the *Sanguine Stream,* near the other world,
Where the dead go to live when we see them no more.

There at *Oke Ironu,* stands a tree mysterious,
With fragrant flowers every day brightly blossoming,
Surrendering in season a thirst-slaking fruit:
That refreshing fruit called Enlightenment.

Those that shall the bank of the *Sanguine Stream* brave,
Those that shall seek the source of its serpentine trail,
Shall there find a mighty gilded portal,
A passage way for the departed, leaving this world,
To the other world where the dead go to live.

At threshold to this grim portal,
There Death has built his somber mansion,

And Pestilence, his consort has planted a flourishing garden.
Ours is therefore a voyage fit only for the valiant,
A pilgrimage for those that will without fear accost Death;
We are valiant men - thirty-six warriors, who have conquered fear,
Resolved to bring to back to our disillusioned city, *Alupayida*;
The thirst-quenching fruit of that tree, called *Enlightenment;*
Which stands in the midst of *Oke Ironu,* that distant city,
Where questions quickly turn into wisdom.

Thirty-six valiant men by many battles made strong,
The brave volunteers to this quest, I should here their virtues extol,
And of their glorious achievements I, *Irinkerindo* must speak;
Though the length of the day, will not this endless tale permit,
And the shortness of the night makes for more prudent use.

I, *Irinkerindo,* tireless seeker after adventure,
Persistently pursuing after the truth wherever it may be found,
For the sake that posterity might thus be made wiser.

Persistently pursuing integrity wherever it may be found,
That the old may marvel at their wealth of wisdom,
Before they sleep and also depart away,
To the other world, where the dead go to live.

Of this journey we falter not nor fear,
Though to our homes we may never again return,
Though we may perish and forever be lost,
Into that land which lies across the *Sanguine Stream*,
To the east of Oke *Ironu*, near that other world,
Where the dead go to live, when we see them no more.

Certainly, shall we on our journey encounter,
Monsters and demons that shall make the heart of men to fail;
Certainly, we shall meet also with terrible fiends,
Which make even the heart of demons to fail;
Mayhap, *Elegbara* will himself cross our path,
That malevolent twin brother to the infernal devil;
With ten thousands of his terrible offspring going forth before,
Warning any that has ears, of his terrible coming.

Thirty-six valiant men whose hearts have murdered fear,
Ceasing to consider Death with his grim appearing;
We voyage toward the distant city of *Oke Ironu*,

Beyond the fearsome forest of *Elegbeje*,
By the slumberous river separated from the other world,
Where the dead go to live, when we see them no more.

Of the brave volunteers to this valiant pursuit,
I, *Irinkerindo* should sing many sweet ballads,
Proclaiming aloud their glorious antecedents;
And though time ceaselessly races forth,
In a dozen years my songs of them shall still not end.

Of *Kumodiran* the brutal one I shall sing:
He that must daily at dawn by heavy cudgels be pummeled,
Else infirmity shall fall upon his body,
And all day will he ceaselessly protest his comfort.

Kumodiran, of whom rumors are rife,
Of his conception from the tempestuous wedlock,
Of the mighty elephant and the brave leopard;
Fearless in pursuit, fearless in defense,
Fearless of any, he personifies our strengths.

Thirty-six valiant men, journeying forth from disenchantment;
Avowed to return with that thirst-quenching fruit,
From the tree which in the middle of *Oke Ironu* stands,

Beyond the distant city: *Oke Langbodo* .
Avowed to return with that fruit called
Enlightenment,
That *Alupayida* may eat and become wise.

THE JOURNEY

We have journeyed many fields and forests,
Where fiery demons and fearsome djinns cavort;
We have swum through sticky rivers alongside treacherous fishes,
And serpentine creatures which devours flesh of men to death.
Indomitable men of valour, resolute in pursuit,
Only of Enlightenment shall our thirst be slaked.

Polycephalous pythons that speak with fiery tongues,
And flesh-eating banshees that wail by night;
Frightening kingdoms of vampire birds which cry like pealing thunder;
We have overcome by sheer might and stubborn boldness.

We have conquered the treacherous *Hila-Hilo* mountains,
Ascended breathless to their lofty peaks,
And without care waded their perilous valleys;
With our glistening swords we have struck off into the dust,
Heads of a hundred barb-toothed mutant ostriches;
We valiant men, resolute in pursuit.

How much our journey should have profited,
By *Kako*, that hunter of legend revived,
With his terrible cudgel struck from a leopard's jaws;
By which fearsome beasts have been by his hands slain,
But alas, he did perish in previous pursuits,
In past travails of the city of Oke *Langbodo*.

How much our journey should have been made smooth,
By *Akara-Ogun*, that hunter of legend revived;
A thousand charms from upon his coat hanging,
By which many foes have been charmed to surrender.
Their hearts paralysed with astonishing fear,
So much that their hairy buttocks turn to water.
But he too alas, did also perish,
In past battles of the city of Oke *Langbodo*.

The road before though presents a perplexing mystery,
For we have found it deep within the thorny wilderness,
Of dark *Irunmole* where the treasures of progenitors,
Lay forever hidden never to be uncovered,
By eyes that only search in idleness.
For *Irunmole* the sacred repository of mysterious runes;
Reveals only by the scriptures of *Orunmila*,
In words spoken of sixteen sacred pebbles.

Before us within that terrible forest *Irunmole*,
Kept by ten thousand fire-breathing demons huge and tiny,
Which roasts the carcasses of fools, astride hot glowing coal by night,
Lay a road mysterious, a beaten track enigmatic.
Have we then found a place of sojourn, in this place that beckons?
Have we then found a place of rest,
In this place where the beaten path before us leads?

Our pursuit urges that we must hasten away,
For the road is twain split, one departing in an unkempt way,
Overgrown with brambles and thorns,
Certainly not of sensible pursuits;
Another departing askew in a tended path,
Kept and prepared for the wise at heart.

But away from this road of thorns *Ifa* instructs us march,
Though with our ready swords, we wish to hack on,
Through the prickly jungle vines; through venom-spitting serpents;
With our poisoned arrows pierce the heart of fearful chimeras,
Which malevolently frolic by the wayside seeking flesh for spoil.

Our urgent pursuit advises to hasten on; to our
destination *Oke Ironu*.

Neither grain nor speck of fear, we have upon us,
Our destination urgently calls, upon us, brave men;
Girdled with battle charms of fourteen hundred
warriors;
That even the seven-headed demons,
Of the wild flee our approaching.
But by this alternate path of brambles and thorns,
The oracle instructs that we yet travel not,
And for a while we must definitely tarry,
In this place where the smooth road leads.

Aching feet from troubles and toil seek respite,
Weary from the arduous ascent of the *Hila-Hilo*
mountains,
And from precarious travels through woods and
fields.
The trampled path, indeed a blissful bed promises,
Away from marauding beasts that prowl unfettered,
The trampled path before, the comfort of a fire by
night promises.
We must therefore for a while rest our weapons,
We must for a while shed our heavy instruments of
war.

Ireke , our trusty bard, bring out you magic flute,

And play a mellow reveille, for here we must indeed tarry,
From the tiresome toil, and of our lengthy travel.

Surely this beaten road shall lead to the city of *Edidare*,
So declares the tired signpost that stands astride the confluence;
Here in *Edidare* we must therefore sojourn,
Here in *Edidare* – where *Gongosu* is king,
And by all his name is known as Omugodimeji.

ÈDÌDÀRÉ

Gullied streets,
By aggregated garbage obliterated;
Geriatrics,
Resolutely peddling tired wares, from hoary heads;
Sinewy youths,
Lying listless in the bosom of Ennui;
As sundry diseases,
Fearlessly roam the streets.

Flies flying festively,
Foraging their putrid meals;
Contemptuous.
Fetid streams of water,
Soiled by soil of the unchaste,
In ragged rivulets flowing
Through the evil heaps;

Multitudes,
Roaming with mind askew,
And scab-spangled bodies biennially washed;
Proudly display injured limbs,
With weeping sores,
Like prized badges of honor.

This is the picture of *Edidare*,

Where *Gongosu* is king and his name is *Omugodimeji*.

Though we must needlessly tarry as the oracle demands,
Wisdom implores that we make our camp away,
From afar off observe, else the ravaging pestilence,
Should endanger the pursuit of our primal mission,
And concatenate our voyage,
To find sop for the ills,
Of our native country *Alupayida*.

Dark clouds overhang heavy heads by sadness bowed,
And despondency is etched on tired faces like stubborn scabs.
A multitude of lethargic youths they thronged,
Imploring that we take them with us away,
Because this place is evil and horrid they wailed;
The future is only of anguish and of hopelessness,
And of inglorious interment, in the belly of the idle.
For their gardens pantries do those in this place of wickedness make,
And stock with stiff corpses of freshly dead siblings,
For feasting on at dinner when the dark night falls.

A desperate youths his name *Iponjudiran*,
Before us fell on his knees wailing and weeping,
Blood from rheumy eyes and cankered sores dripping,
And boils on his body, lumpy as river pebbles.

Of his ailments and pains *Iponjudiran* cried,
And wept for his mother at home, *Surulekan*;
Twenty four months pregnant and for fear,
Of the grimness, of the life awaiting,
Would not yield the child, to a cruel world.

Iponjudiran wept;
For loved siblings, a few days deceased,
In hideous rigor, waiting in the garden,
To be food to the living,
Who wait to die.
For in *Edidare* the loss of friend brings gastronomic joy,
And the death of foes causes the belly to roar in ecstasy.
Life is here bereft of other purpose,
Than a ritual, of cannibalistic pleasures.

Iponjudiran wept for his father *Iforiti*,
Who in confusion at home sits,
In doldrums of insanity,
Tired of living; afraid of dying.

For the depth of his grief we thus followed him,
That perhaps by our presence we may his loved ones give hope;
Verily, he imagines a spirit of benevolence with us walks.

There found we *Iforiti* laid on bed of sodden leaves,
Snow-white head on grey slab of rock pillowed -
This being the sanity that their wisdom had afforded,
This being the custom of these strange people,
Edidare.

There found we *Surulekan* groaning and crying,
For the pains of the womb were violent and unceasing,
Yet would she not yield her precious burden,
For in this place *Edidare* the dead feed the living,
And those unborn no more than mere meat,
Stored away in warm larders,
Waiting for ravenous jaws.

Of sparse knowledge did we encourage those that suffered:
From the woods gathered herbs, leaves and roots,
For poultices and ointments for festering sores,
For soothing tonics to assuage diverse ailments.
And daily did we thereafter seek *Surulekan*,
With words of compassion, soothing her pains.

Alas, *Iforiti* soon ascended to his ancestors,
In comfort though that hope had at in *Edidare* berthed,
To the woods we there buried him,
Far from the joyful stomachs of slavering neighbours.
Iponjudiran also, we took with us,

Far from the evil stench of this place, *Edidare*.

For reasons of the filth and evil stench,
Which makes the eyes saddened and sorrowed,
Which makes the heart to be distressed and sorely aggrieved,
We thought and resolved to seek the king,
Who rules over this expanse of dreadful squalor,
That we might worship his lack of wisdom,
That we may marvel upon his unfortunate insignificance.

Surely atop of a heap of dung,
There must preside a *busy-ness* of pestilent flies,
There must preside, one exalted royal vermin,
On scum patinaed throne, demanding reverence.

They die by the dozens these hapless people,
Daily of ghastly illnesses and lethal sloth,
For sake of conscience we must therefore seek,
Gongosu the great king of *Edidare*,
Who by all is known as *Omugodimeji*.

Emissaries we therefore sent to *Gongosu*,
Bearing greetings of friendly sojourners,
And gifts that we might purchase of him a listening ear.
Thus were we by the king invited into his royal court,
Thus with joyful anger, we prepared to meet *Gongosu*.

Alas by morning we receive distressing news:
With hoe over his shoulder, and machete in hand,
Gongosu had to his farm traveled away by dawn,
To toil and to bring food for ten wives,
For his fifty children and seventy servants,
Who still in the palace lie in blissful sleep,
As the cock had yet crowed only thrice.

When shall Gongosu from this foolish task return?
By nightfall word again returned to us.
That the king will in his court receive us, when morning comes.
Alas, next morning again came word from *Gongosu*,
Of weariness from the burden of victuals,
Which he had from the royal farm borne upon his back,
To feed ten wives, fifty children and seventy servants.
For two days *Gongosu* must thus rest,
Before he can with us, have audience in the royal court.

Alas, to the royal farm, *Gongosu* had again the appointed day journeyed,
For the food which on his back he bore two days before,
Sufficed not for all that lived in the palace;
Thus off to work the king again must go,
Off to the royal farm far away *Gongosu* must go,
To toil for food, that his servants must be fed.

The tasks that stared us are very enormous,
Thousands cry to be delivered from their ailments,
A multitude seeks to be awakened into new hope;
Shall we then haplessly seek a fugitive king?

As the wounds of *Iponjudiran* healed,
With him we endeavored we to cultivate vast farms,
Planted fruits and vegetables and reared livestock,
Of which he should feed and sell for profit.

Hordes of the forlorn youths we gathered,
Their strengths they unleashed upon the fallow forests,
Planting mighty plantations, orchards and cattle pens,
Ceasing to be bereft of hope,

The dead and the rotting of *Edidare* they took away,
Deep in the forest *Irunmole,* they buried the dead.
Thus stank *Edidare* less, though the garbage remained strong:
For decades it had gathered and now petrified.

The strong youth we taught to weave and to use the awl,
For selves and kin to make new coats and shoes,
For in *Edidare* a family had no more than a single dress,
Worn each on their body by daily rotation,

For reason therefore had the children needlessly died,
Of grievous ailments that ride on humid winds.

Many days did we earnestly wait,
While *Gongosu* tirelessly toiled, his wives to make fat,
While *Gongosu* worked all day his servants to keep content.
Our joy was great on the seventeenth day of our sojourn,
Gongosu at last awaits us, news arrived;
To the palace of the king at *Edidare,* we thus hasted
To the palace with ancient fence .two feet high,
To the palace with walls of crumbling mud,
To the royal palace with dreary roof sagged heavy with age.

Were if not for a fool sitting astride the fence,
A bolt of cloth about his loins, a tall cap upon his head,
In disgust would we have returned to camp,
We despaired that there will be more than despondency and futility,
Behind those hideous crumbling walls,
Of the palace of *Gongosu,* king of *Edidare,*
Who by all is called by name, *Omugodimeji.*

Nevertheless did we venture to ask the fool,
Seated atop the crumbling fence of the royal palace,
Where we may go, to find the king of *Edidare.*

Who is called by name, *Omugodimeji.*

The fool he looked upon us with disdain unhidden,
And asked of us, what purpose we seek the king.
But this fool we declined to answer mayhap,
As is the custom of these people he seeks of us a bribe.
In response his eyes glistened with insanity this fool,
And for the assault of a maniac we girded ourselves.

From within the palace came a fellow running,
And upon his face reverently fall before this fool on the fence,
Hail the king! Hail the king!; the prostrate servant worshiped,
Thus did we begin to think in utter ignorance,
Mayhap such is how the king's vassals worship one another,
In this place, of awesome confusion, Edidare,
Where *Gongosu* is king and his name is *Omugodimeji.*

This fellow which lay on the ground worshiping,
He pointed a timid finger at us berating our ignorance,
And the blindness of our eyes, which had failed to discern,
The king who sits naked before us, on the palace wall,
A sheet of cloth about his loins; a long cap on his head.

Thus also was *Gongosu* at our presence doubly angered.

Surprised, I fell therefore upon the ground,
Worshipping the king, the great *Gongosu* of *Edidare*
Hail, hail *Gongosu*; hail, hail *Omugodimeji*,
Belly to the ground, his forgiveness I pleaded,
That our mission might yet be salvaged.

In unrelenting anger *Omugodimeji* railed,
Indeed we were blind buffoons unable to discern,
A great king regally perched upon his palace fence.
A piece of cloth on his waist and a cap upon his head;
And had our eyes not completely failed us,
Had we been born with even a smattering of understanding,
Does not the magnificent crown, upon the head of *Gongosu*,
Surpass all crowns in this world in beauty,
And not sufficiently hinted of majesty?

Is there a city more glorious in beauty than *Edidare*?
Ever in this world had any seen an edifice,
Of greater beauty than the palace of *Gongosu*,
King of *Edidare*, whose name is *Omugodimeji*?
Ever has there lived one wiser than the great *Gongosu*?

O abject fools be warned of the anger of Gongosu,
Lest in your sojourn in this glorious city Edidare,

The wrath of Omugodimeji you bring upon your foolish heads.

Great confusion we found amongst us,
That *Omugodimeji* truly thought without a hint of doubt,
That *Edidare* was indeed very great and mighty,
O what a great and terrible calamity,
For the fool who imagines self wise remains indeed,
To all that watch the greatest dunce in the world:
Even as he denies his blundering buffoonery,
Wisdom firmly flees from his pitiable presence.

With pleasant words at last I stood forth to speak,
With flattery sweet as honey, and with the tongue of a crafty praise singer,
Though *Ayederu-Eda*, the bard behind me stood consumed by anger,
His gift of contrivance and intrigue for once fleeing him.

Thus spoke I to the king *Gongosu*,
Of our delight with this mighty and beautiful city *Edidare*,
How honoured we were to stand in the king's presence,
Though on a crumbling fence he sits, while the city rots and stinks.
Thus spoke I to the king *Gongosu*:

Fret not therefore Gongosu that we failed to worship you,
For indeed are we merely ignorant oafs,
Blind to this greatness which before us sits,
For much travel has our eyes cloyed with tiredness.

Thus did I implore *Gongosu* against his burning wrath,
Pacified *Omugodimeji* that he might become our friend,
That we may be free guests to the king's magnificent palace,
And to *Gongosu* bring many gifts in reverence,
For nowhere but Edidare is there such great and wonderful splendor.

Ayederu-Eda :
The magic bard, the great praise singer,
Gifted in contrivance and in words of intrigue,
By my elegant flattering grossly bewildered,
With laughing eyes for my resourcefulness saluted.

Kumodiran:
That one of violent words and deeds,
Upon *Gongosu* unleashed anger strong as a roaring whirlwind,
Told of his sadness to behold so great a fool,
Who with a mad mind makes merry boast,
Of such astounding perfidy,
As a city filled with rotting corpses,
And garbage heaps standing tall as mansions.

O Gongosu you sit on the fence and dream of greatness,
While all around there lies only death and destruction,
And your sparse royal garments proudly demonstrates,
The laughable garbs of a blustering clown.

We come to you with hearts heavy with concern,
And if today your ears have not yet failed you must listen,
Though mere words indeed should fail to describe this abominable city,
And in foulness never will there be another to surpass Edidare.
We have to you with sound counsel and good reason come, O Gongosu,
And listen you must for we shall nevertheless speak.

But strongly did I warn *Kumodiran* to desist from this harangue,.
That we are not suddenly cast into battle with *Edidare*,
But *Gongosu* responding with laughter as loud as thunder,
Fell from the fence and in the dust rolled with glee.
His servant he charged to lead us into the palace,
Where *Gongosu* will this day have royal audience,
With the valiant men, in pursuit of Enlightenment.

THE KING'S PALACE

Wives and concubines in nakedness roam and saunter,
In speech and comportment utterly unchaste:
In the palace of *Gongosu* consternation reigns,

The disgusting nakedness of the corpulent queen,
We nevertheless followed in a tour of the palace,
Through rooms, treasury, kitchens and toilets, she led us,
And even of all things not meant to be known she enlightened us,

By this indiscreet woman were our eyes and ears so sorrowed,
That we implored her kindly ,say nothing more,
Not about king, servants, mistresses nor cattle;
But recalcitrant, she persisted declaring,
That upon her tongue, the wish of *Gongosu* must prevail.
For even as she does speak, so had *Gongosu* commanded her do.

Released at last from this buffoonery we sat,
In the king's concourse impatiently waiting his presence,
That we might at last place our mission before him,

That we might before him place our concern for
Edidare.

Even as *Gongosu* sat before us there came a servant,
The yam is cooked and the kitchen awaits the king,
To pound the yam that is cooked, said the servant,
For the entire palace impatiently await their meal at noon.

Thus did Omugodimeji haste away to toil in the kitchen,
Instructing nevertheless that we speak with his trusted counselor,
Who three generations of *Gongosu* before him had served,
And beside the throne on the right hand sits he always,
His name as known to all generations: *Atanpako*.

Atanpako sat grumpy,
As a portly vulture coldly regarding carrion,
And looking upon us with baleful eyes,
A countenance surly as of a bloated toad,
Upon us croaked to declare our mission.

Thus spoke I to *Atanpako* the king's counselor,
Of the heaps of filth,
Of the horde of vermin,
Of the virulent diseases,

Which in *Edidare*, daily caused needless death.
Of the evil of drinking soiled water,
Of the perverted pleasure of eating carrion,
I spoke.

Should the people ventilate their musty homes,
Should they wear dry clothes and sleep in dry beds;
Should the people daily make selves clean in the river,
Death shall less seldom wait at the threshold of homes,
And from them disease shall be held in strong fetters.

Thus did I say to the counselor *Atanpako*,
His hoary head he nodded as though in accord,
A withered thumb he raised as if in agreement.

A cry of consternation and word came to all,
That the king with his youngest wife wrestled in the kitchen,
And this place of the newest confusion,
Found we *Gongosu* in the dust upon his back,
His wife *Werediran* upon his chest perched,
And with heavy hands bludgeoned him upon the face.
But with heavier hands did we rescue *Gongosu* from certain death,
From the hands of this frail woman who with him wrestled.

Alas, *Gongosu* arose and again made loud boast,
Of how the rude woman, he would have taught the lesson of her life;
And again from our hands *Werediran* escaped,
And in the twinkling of the eye launched again upon *Gongosu*.
Again did *Omugodimeji* lay splayed in the dust,
Again did we rescue *Gongosu*, from this frail woman.

Seven times did this quarrelsome woman *Werediran*,
Make *Gongosu* a foot mat and a public disgrace,
Before kith, kin, servants and strangers looking on ,very entertained.
After the seventh time in fear fled *Omugodimeji*.
With *Werediran* the daughter of *Agbako-tunji*,
Around the palace grounds pursuing, on dainty feet.

A sorry sight to see indeed was *Gongosu*,
Rescued at last from this dreadful and mortifying encounter,
From head to toe covered in dust and filth,
And in exhaustion he gasped for breath like a dying beast.

O Gongosu, she did not beat you so much today,
Said a servant to *Gongosu* king of *Edidare*,
I am now beginning to understand how she fights,
And nearly today did I conquer her.
Replied *Gongosu* with pride aglow.

Where is your crown, O Gongosu?
Inquired another servant, in great mirth.
I do not know, where it is
Mayhap the stream has taken it away
Even as I fell in the flowing water.
Thus replied *Gongosu* with pride aglow.

She is indeed a terrible woman; Werediran,
And my skull she would have broken into little shards,
Even as her mother did to her unfortunate father,
And till this day her mother is kept in prison.
My wife is from a family of murderers, I tell you all
But can you not see that she is indeed so beautiful?
Even though she herself,
Has three times been kept in prison,
Till I took her as wife for she is indeed so beautiful-
Tall, elegant and a joy to the discerning eyes.

She certainly would to you appear skilled in wrestling,
But mark you all, I Gongosu am the master of Werediran,
And if once more she comes to challenge me,
Then to an inch of her life I shall I certainly trash her,
For now I now know all the fighting tricks of Werediran.

So declared *Gongosu* to all gathered,
So said *Omugodimeji* to the astounded before him gathered.

She comes again! She comes again!
Someone shouted, a loud cry from far away,
And *Gongosu* away from his palace fled for dear life,
With *Werediran* sprinting behind in mad pursuit.

O *Gongosu*, after the fighting of this day has subsided,
And your bruises and wounds have been washed and salved,
We shall again return tonight, our urgent mission to bare,
For now your garment is in utter tatters,
Tonight we shall again return O *Gongosu*.
And our heartache for *Edidare* we shall then declare.

Rotimi Ogunjobi

THE BETRAYAL OF ATANPAKO

Again at dusk returned we to *Gongosu*,
His strife with wife *Werediran* now abated;
But in long conference found we, him with the counselor *Atanpako*.
Thus again we awaited the audience of *Gongosu*.

Alas, his words were once more in anger as he turned upon us:
Ignorant wanderers foisting lies upon idle ears,
You come to visit me with your contrivances,
And attempt to blind my vision with wily counsel;
But I see your dastardly plot to steal this country Edidare,
By teaching the people strange and alien customs?

Never in my life has it been said that the pox is bad,
Is it not by disease that the body is strengthened?
Fetch me, you lying deceivers a fellow struck with the pox,
And him I will lovingly cuddle to my bosom and make my friend.

Filth is good and pleasant for it speaks of abundance,
And a house bereft of windows,
Rather makes for a warmer bed.
Not for another minute shall I listen to your wily counsel.
For I perceive a trick to steal this great country Edidare

Edidare

Askance we looked upon counselor *Atanpako*,
Desiring of him to speak a word in favour,
Against this great delusion of *Gongosu*,
But *Atanpako* against our presence hardened his face,
And turning to *Gongosu* a gnarled thumb he raised.

From the palace we departed, by *Atanpako* utterly betrayed,
 From the palace of *Gongosu* of *Edidare*:
Surpassed in wisdom, only by utter foolishness.

Six days after did we again return hopeful,
Again sought *Gongosu*, mayhap of his folly he has repented,
Alas, we found *Gongosu* struck ill of a strange disease,
Omugodimeji groaned upon his bed in throes of death,
Which dutifully seven days after did at last come.

If kings would learn to heed wise counsel,
And be not obstinate in their single perceptions;
If kings will hearken to good and sound counsel,
And bend their ears to contrary voices,
Then are cities, made great and mighty,
Then are people made strong and wealthy.

Into the forest we took *Omugodimeji* and there him we interred,
Even as his entire salivated in the expectation,
Of his juicy laps roasting on hot coals,

Of his belly on a spittle dripping fat,
Onto a crackling bed of burning wood.

OMUGODIMETA

Great hopes we had placed upon *Edidare*,
That a new dawn now finally shall arrive,
For a new king shall indeed now be crowned,
Gongosu,
Even as *Omugodimeji* has to his ancestors ascended.

On the seventh day after *Omugodimeji* had departed,
Was crowned his eldest son, his name *Omugodimeta*,
And he feted us, he and his mother *Ilaburu*,
He feted us, he and his brother *Danasungbo*.

Upon the ground they fell, on their bellies before us,
Reverently worshipped us sojourners, one after the other,
Thirty-six times in all this family of fools.

And for astuteness did *Omugodimeta* make me chief;
Reverently bestowed a princely title, *Ipakodiwura*.
With grim face and contrived smiles full of poison,
Did *Atanpako* again raise a withered thumb.
But the youth of *Edidare* they rejoiced,
And for us they raised a celebration dance.

Surulekan the mother of *Iponjudiran*,
From her womb at last did release the unborn child,
Into her arms she received a newly born baby,

A beautiful boy over which she long wept for joy,
In endearment to us sojourners, with whom had come hope,
The child she named after me *Irinkerindo*.

Gongo so.
The multitude danced and the drums sang with lustful tongues,
On coronation day when *Omugodimeta* was crowned as king,
A day of great dancing and great cavorting,
Of feasting and mighty speeches uttered without meaning:

May he live forever, the great Omugodimeta,
May he live forever, the great Gongosu- king of Edidare.

The multitude danced and the drums sang with lustful tongues:

Gongosu Edidare, Gongosu Edidare,
Bi o ti gbon to naa lo go to,
Gongosu Edidare, Gongosu Edidare.

O *Gongosu* , O *Gongosu* ,
Your wisdom by your glorious foolishness
Will never ever, fail to be surpassed.

THE COURT OF EDIDARE

The day comes, and *Gongosu* must preside,
Over the court of *Edidare*,
Where the people are judged.
The day comes, and *Gongosu* must preside,
Over the court of *Edidare*,
Where the laws are crafted.
And me *Ipakodiwura*,
Omugodimeta had invited to observe,

Thus prepared *Omugodimeta*,
To preside over *Opitanparapo:*
The noble gathering where the people are judged,
And the laws of the land made.

And *Omugodimeta* implored that I follow,
That I may see,
How well *Gongosu* shall judge his people;
Also that his new counselor, *Ipakodiwura* he might present,
To approval of the gathering of *Opitanparapo* .

Two new horses have I purchased,
And they are the finest steed in the world,
One I shall ride while you ride upon the other.
Thus said to me *Gongosu*, king of *Edidare*

Great was my amazement when his steeds were brought:
Two cows, with madness frothing by the mouth.
Mayhap *Gongosu* was blind or his servants insane,
So did I explain that these are cows and not horses.

They laughed, and scorned me, both king and servants,
These beasts, they insist are what they call horses,
Here in *Edidare* where *Gongosu* is King,
And his name is known as *Omugodimeta*.

Fearful nevertheless of the expectable danger,
Did I decline to mount upon the back of a cow.
But *Gongosu* , utterly fearless in his great foolishness,
Atop his cow leapt and by the horn grappled with the beast.
Mad with its fear the cow tossed *Gongosu* into the dust,
And with its horns would have gored *Gongosu* to death,
Had I not with a stick beaten the furious beast away.
But *Omugodimeta*, fearless in astounding foolishness,
Onto the back of his enraged cow again he leapt,
And off and away cantered king and angry beast,
With great hue and cries, following down the dusty road.

Edidare

At the court of *Opitanparapo*,
Where the people are judged, and the laws are made;
In *Edidare*,
Where *Gongosu* is king and his name is *Omugodimeta*;
Needed I not to have been ashamed,
Of the king's ludicrous steed,
For many had come also
Riding voracious cockroaches,
And many had come astride,
Ravenous wriggling caterpillars.

Opitanparapo, a gathering in bedlam:
Where the people are judged, and laws crafted.
A noble gathering in drunken chat and blind banter lost;
Unmindful even of the coming of the king.
Opitanparapo, a gathering in bedlam:

Thus *Gongosu*, he raised his voice,
Aloud *Omugodimeta* cried for all to hear,
Aloud *Gongosu*, roared aloud that time had come l
To recite the great creed of the noble gathering
Opitanparapo.

At last came the multitude to silence and attention,
And with hand over breast rose to their feet,
In unison chanting the glorious creed of *Opitanparapo*:

I believe in food, master of the body
Good food makes for a good and healthy body,
Makes strong bones and enriches the blood,
Unwholesome food invites disease to the body,
And makes the body frail, weak and even to die,
I believe in food, I believe in food
I believe in good food, clean water, fresh air,
For these entire make for a healthy body.
I believe in food, I believe in food
  Amen.

By surprise was I thoroughly shaken,
Though *Edidare* stank in filth, disease and death,
The worth of good victuals was not here a knowledge lacked,
Enough they knew to make a national creed.

Such a great mystery was in a moment explained,
For the creed preceded the first in the lineage of *Gongosu*,
When wise kings ruled had the creed been crafted.

Alas, in our sojourn we had also lost a valiant man:
Ibembe-Olokunrun, the one of avaricious appetite,
Who by desires of his stomach been lured away,
And to the savagery of Edidare had lost his soul.

Ibembe-Olokunrun whom I had found a hermit,
Making his dwelling of a cave in the hills,

Ibembe-Olokunrun of whom been well warned,
For indeed he was the greatest glutton in the world.

Ibembe-Olokunrun whom at his lair I had found in the hills,
Two dead antelopes spread before him in a feast,
And from these did he feverishly feast, deaf to my approaching,
Though several times his name I had cried aloud,
And not for a minute had *Ibembe-Olokunrun* heeded my callings,
Till his feast, he had flesh and bones completely devoured.

By the promise of a forest full of flesh,
Had I engaged the heart of *Ibembe-Olokunrun* into our quest;
Alas, by the promise of a feast more plentiful,
Had *Edidare* stolen the heart of our valiant warrior.

Amidst *Opitanparapo* now stood *Ibembe-Olokunrun,*
Demanding of the gathering that discussion be urgently begun,
Regarding what should hence be done with the dead,
For *Edidare* now eat a diet of fruit and vegetables,
Brought from fields that the youth had planted;
Demanding of the gathering that discussion be urgently begun,
Of the dead that wasted away in the gardens, uneaten.

Perhaps it may be profitable, he declared- *Ibembe-Olokunrun,*
To sell the dead bodies away,
To far off cities for their dinner tables,
Mayhap it could be also of profit to sell away the aged,
That they arrive freshly dead for the tables in far way lands,
Mayhap it could be even prudent, he argued *Ibembe-Olokunrun,*
To eat the suckling babies and defenseless young children,
Before they grow up and ripen into blemished adults,
Unfit for sale for the dinner tables in far away lands.
Surely by this commerce should *Edidare* prosper,
And for lovingly reared family the people justly rewarded.
And for *Ibembe-Olokunrun* all *Opitanparapo* rose,
And to this great wisdom raised a loud ovation.

Indulged to speak, I stood appalled,
Told all gathered how evil it was to eat kindred flesh,
And were they not so blind then should they not know,
That never do beasts eat kindred beast;
Lions do not feed on lions, nor leopards on leopards,
And even the detestable vulture
Would never on kindred carrion bird feed.

More dignifying, the commerce that comes of hard work,
Of crops planted in season and animals with care tended,
And of youths engaged in productive toil,
For eating people is bad.

By these words were they in shame made briefly mute,
And to this matter resolved they to return on a better day.
Upon the back *Gongosu* proudly patted me *Ipakodiwura*,
And publicly did he for my astuteness congratulate me.

Two cases there were, for the king to judge;
Two cases both for which *Gongosu* stood defendant.
A knave, *Inaki-takiti* had three of *Gongosu's* wives,
Purloined, and into own house quartered away;
Today before *Gongosu* had come all three stolen women,
To bring the king to a judgment of divorce;
Cursing, abusing and utterly unmindful,
That the case will be judged by the defendant the king,
That judgment will be meted by *Gongosu* of *Edidare*.

Alas, before them fell *Gongosu* on his knees pleading;
Imploring three stolen wives return again;
But *Inaki-takiti* for the fugitive wives resolutely raised an angry petition,
And to *Gongosu* returned the dowry paid for three stolen wives.
The sum of which in total came to three pence;
For a wife comes for a penny in *Edidare*,
Where *Gongosu* is king and his name is *Omugodimeta*.

Again came another petition, for which Gongosu, stood accused:
About the departed king *Omugodimeji* a creditor had come railing,
Of how *Omugodimeji* had died with four pence unpaid debt;
Which before the court *Osomalo* had in earnest come demanding,
If violence should be avoided *Gongosu*,
Even in the midst of this exalted gathering.

So took *Gongosu* of the three pence regained dowry,
Paid him by *Inaki-takiti* for release of three stolen wives,
And to *Osomalo*, creditor to his father *Omugodimeji* gave three pence,
That violence shall be avoided *Gongosu* even in this exalted gathering.
Of *Opitanparapo* , where *Gongosu* is king,

And is by all known by name, Omugodimeta.

Alas, the debt paid was a penny short of being redeemed,
At which *Osomalo* in anger cried and further railed,
And made vicious threats to have *Gongosu* thrown in jail,
For the debt was still one penny short,
Of what is owed by his dead father *Omugodimeji*.

Again knelt the king and in desperation implored,
For *Gongosu* had not a penny to pay to redeem the debt,
Owed *Osomalo* by his father *Omugodimeji*;
So was *Gongosu* in public admonished:
If in three day the debt of one penny still subsisted,
Owed *Osomalo* by his father *Omugodimeji*,
Certainly shall *Gongosu* be committed to prison,
From where he shall for the rest of his life rule as king.

For a friendly face did *Omugodimeta* desperately search,
From amongst the amused gathering of *Opitanparapo*,
But away all looked unconcerned for his sorry plight,
None would lend *Omugodimeta* a penny to pay the debt,
Owed *Osomalo* by his father *Omugodimeji*.

Angered, from my pocket took I one penny,
To *Osomalo* gave the penny that *Gongosu* shall not languish in jail,
For reason of a delinquent debt of one single penny,
Owed *Osomalo* by his dead father *Omugodimeji*.
Upon the back again *Gongosu* proudly patted me,
And for great generosity *Omugodimeta* mightily congratulated me.

Nay, we shall nevertheless eat the dead.
In fury stood *Atanpako* to declare,
Gnarled finger accused and eyes burned as fiery coals,
This spy comes again with his strange devices,
By which same he did lead Omugodimeji to needless death,
Having taken captive the mind of the people in rebellious toil.

Therefore, custodians of the traditions of Edidare, beware,
That he does not confuse Opitanparapo with his dangerous wiles,
And imprison your minds in his beguiling ways,
Soon leading Edidare into captivity of coming invaders.
I implore you therefore Opitanparapo
Bear no more of this knave's chicanery
Else Edidare would be forever lost to marauders.

Strong and damning were *Atanpako*'s fiery words against me,
And a long silence they brought to the gathering of *Opitanparapo*,

Uncertain they looked upon me and upon one another,
Till turncoat *Ibembe-Olokunrun* ordered that I be expelled,
From the town of *Edidare* forever banished.
In assent Atanpako raised a withered thumb;
So did many more for there were others as him.
Thus did *Gongosu* himself wave me a forlorn farewell.

Great sadness was mine, that *Gongosu* so easily had acquiesced,
That *Gongosu* should for my generosity turn so easily away,
But a fool it is said shall forever remain,
Though dressed up in the garbs of the greatest sage.

Persistent, *Atanpako* again in his evil ways,
Against me caused two troubling decrees to be by *Gongosu* raised,
To strike at my peace and to cause me great distress:

Hear ye, hear ye; all the world, hear ye;
Anyone who sets their eyes upon Irinkerindo, the king of bandits,
Must with a heavy pole clobber him upon the back,
Else, such transgressor, whether man or woman,
Shall pay an instant fine, of five pence.

Thus said the first decree, and it is clearly utter wickedness,
That *Gongosu* who could not a debt of one penny pay,
Now decrees a greater penalty of five pence,
For any who fails with a stick to batter me;
A punishment of five pence,
The price of five women in *Edidare;*
Where *Gongosu* is king,
And his name is *Omugodimeta,*

Hear ye, hear ye; all the world hear ye;
All who seeks to sojourn in this country Edidare,
Must eat of our foods, and drink of our water,
They must live in our houses
Else go to prison for ten minutes.

Thus said the second decree;
And to these decrees, declared Gongosu:

This to law have I signed
With my hand, my feet, my eyes
My nose, my head, my neck,
My front, my back, my teeth,
My tongue, my nostril, my ear;

I, Gongosu, the greatest king in the world
The great Omugodimeta, king of Edidare,
Son of my father Omugodimeji,
Son of my mother Ilaburu,

Brother to my brother Danasungbo

On this day of the sixth month,
Of the year Two thousand and thirteen.
After the death of our Lord:
The only one ever wiser than me, Omugodimeta.

Rotimi Ogunjobi

THE DEPARTURE

We leave *Edidare* not for fear but for peace,
For we, thirty-six warriors great in battle,
Are easily able to sack *Opitanparapo*.
We, thirty-six men of valour and resolve.
Are easily able to end this mindless reign of *Gongosu*,
But peace we thought we must with haste embrace,
Yea, *Ifa* instructs that our journey must again progress.

Edidare, our task is done, we must now depart,
We must at last our sojourn in this sadness end,
Again our mission we must with urgency pursue.

Hearken to us nevertheless, Edidare;
Shall the reign of this dynasty of *Gongosu* perpetuate,
And decadence like a termite nest sits upon the land?
Shall the treacherous cohorts as *Atanpako*,
The ravenous greed as of *Ibembe-Olokunrun*,
And brutal buffoonery as of *Opitanparapo*,
Remain domineering totems,
While far and wide the ground stay scorched?

Farewell   *Edidare* where *Gongosu* is king,
Over the horizon ominous clouds approach,
Bearing a downpour of refreshing enfranchisement,

And the petrified garbage which against your dream stand unyielding,
Shall at last be completely washed away.
Nurture well the seeds which our sojourn has sown in your hearts,
And with hard work thereafter redeem your city from ruin,

Thirty-six men of valour and urgent resolve,
Voyaging to the city where wisdom grows on trees;
Whose fragrant flowers every day rise up in beautiful blossoms,
Yielding to the patient, that thirst-quenching fruit,
Surrendering to the resolute, the fruit of wisdom.

LITERAL TRANSLATIONS

Most of the Yoruba words in the poem are really not in common use. In Yoruba storytelling, names are usually created to describe a person, a situation or to add life to the environment of a story. Some other names such as which are prefixed *Oke* which means *hill*, merely describe the name of a place rather than suggest that there is a clearly visible geological protrusion. They are comparable to English places such as *Notting Hill* or *Crawley Rise*. Nevertheless it is highly probable that at some time in ancient history such a place could have actually been clearly seen as a hill.

Agbako-tunji - (lit.) Demon incarnate. In Yoruba storytelling Agbako, also known as the Spirit of misfortune, is regarded the most terrible demon to encounter.

Akara-Ogun – (lit.) Magic charm. This name would really be a nickname.

Alupayida -Healing herb.

Atanpako – Thumb.

Ayederu-Eda – Dishonest person.

Bi o ti gbon to naa lo go to –You are as wise as you are foolish.

Danasungbo – Unskilled person, imbecile. Often used as an insult.

Elegbara – The devil.
Gongo so – The drumstick spoke. *Gongo* is the name of the crooked drumstick used on the talking-drum.
Gongosu – Absolutely stupid; an idiot. Often used as an insult.
Hila-Hilo – Great trouble; tribulation. Describes situations of extreme hardship.
Iforiti – Perseverance.
Ibembe-Olokunrun – (lit.) Slothful person; indolent glutton. From the way a millipede curls up as if asleep.
Inaki- takiti - (lit.) As frisky as a gorilla.
Ipakodiwura – (lit.) Head as precious as gold.
Iponjudiran – (lit.) Adversity becomes a public spectacle.
Ireke – Sugar cane.
Irinkerindo – Adventure.
Irunmole – Mystical.
Kumodiran – Violence becomes a public spectacle.
Oke Ironu – Contemplation Hill or Rise
Omugodimeji – (lit.) Fool the second (Fool II)
Omugodimeta – (lit.) Fool the third (Fool III)
Opitanparapo – (lit.) The gathering of storytellers.
Osomalo – An itinerant trader from the Ilesha area of Western Nigeria. These traders have a habit of shrewdly giving items on credit and then very soon returning to pester for repayment.
Surulekan - (lit.) Patience plus one. Extra-patient
Werediran – Madness becomes a public spectacle.

About the Author

Rotimi 'Timi' Ogunjobi is publisher of both The Redbridge Review and Lagos Literary and Arts Journal. His many published books include non-fiction, novels, short story collections, plays and poetry.
He is a software engineer, technical author and President of Cognisci ISTD Foundation, an IT development NGO.

Web site: http://www.rotimiogunjobi.me.uk

Other Books by the Author

- A Conference in Ennui
- Brain Surgery on the Highway and other Manic Expressions

Rotimi Ogunjobi

www.ingramcontent.com/pod-product-compliance
Lightning Source LLC
Chambersburg PA
CBHW061513040426
42450CB00008B/1598